DON'T
CALL
US
DEAD

poems

DANEZ
SMITH

Graywolf Press

This publication is made possible, in part, by the voters of Minnesota through a Minnesota State Arts Board Operating Support grant, thanks to a legislative appropriation from the arts and cultural heritage fund, and a grant from the Wells Fargo Foundation. Significant support has also been provided by the Jerome Foundation, the Lannan Foundation, Target, the McKnight Foundation, the Amazon Literary Partnership, and other generous contributions from foundations, corporations, and individuals. To these organizations and individuals we offer our heartfelt thanks.

Published by Graywolf Press
250 Third Avenue North, Suite 600
Minneapolis, Minnesota 55401

www.graywolfpress.org

Published in the United States of America

ISBN 978-1-55597-785-6

2 4 6 8 9 7 5 3 1
First Graywolf Printing, 2017

Library of Congress Control Number: 2017930111

Cover design: Kapo Ng

Cover art: Shikeith, *The moment you doubt whether you can fly, you cease forever to be able to do it*

DON'T CALL US DEAD

Also by Danez Smith

[insert] boy

for Pookie
my day one & best love

Contents

Oh my God, oh my God
If I die, I'm a legend
Drake

he who wore death discourages any plague
Sonia Sanchez

summer, somewhere

somewhere, a sun. below, boys brown
as rye play the dozens & ball, jump

in the air & stay there. boys become new
moons, gum-dark on all sides, beg bruise

-blue water to fly, at least tide, at least
spit back a father or two. i won't get started.

history is what it is. it knows what it did.
bad dog. bad blood. bad day to be a boy

color of a July well spent. but here, not earth
not heaven, we can't recall our white shirts

turned ruby gowns. here, there's no language
for *officer* or *law*, no color to call *white*.

if snow fell, it'd fall black. please, don't call
us dead, call us alive someplace better.

we say our own names when we pray.
we go out for sweets & come back.

　　/ /

this is how we are born: come morning
after we cypher/feast/hoop, we dig

a new one from the ground, take
him out his treebox, shake worms

from his braids. sometimes they'll sing
a trapgod hymn (what a first breath!)

sometimes it's they eyes who lead
scanning for bonefleshed men in blue.

we say *congrats, you're a boy again!*
we give him a durag, a bowl, a second chance.

we send him off to wander for a day
or ever, let him pick his new name.

that boy was Trayvon, now called *RainKing*.
that man Sean named himself *i do, i do*.

O, the imagination of a new reborn boy
but most of us settle on *alive*.

//

sometimes a boy is born
right out the sky, dropped from

a bridge between starshine & clay.
one boy showed up pulled behind

a truck, a parade for himself
& his wet red train. years ago

we plucked brothers from branches
peeled their naps from bark.

sometimes a boy walks into his room
then walks out into his new world

still clutching wicked metals. some boys
waded here through their own blood.

does it matter how he got here if we're all here
to dance? grab a boy! spin him around!

if he asks for a kiss, kiss him.
if he asks where he is, say *gone*.

    //

dear air where you used to be, dear empty Chucks
by front door, dear whatever you are now, dear son

they buried you all business, no ceremony.
cameras, t-shirts, essays, protests

then you were just dead. some nights
i want to dig you up, bury you right.

scrape dirt until my hands are raw
& wounds pack themselves with mud.

i want to dig you up, let it rain twice
before our next good-bye.

dear sprinkler dancer, i can't tell if I'm crying
or i'm the sky, but praise your sweet rot

unstitching under soil, praise dandelions
draining water from your greening, precious flesh.

i'll plant a garden on top
where your hurt stopped.

11

just this morning the sun laid a yellow not-palm
on my face & i woke knowing your hands

were once the only place in the world.
this very morning i woke up

& remembered unparticular Tuesdays
my head in your lap, scalp covered in grease

& your hands, your hands, those hands
my binary gods. Those milk hands, bread hands

hands in the air in church hands, cut-up fish hands
for my own good hands, back talk backhands, hurt more

than me hands, ain't asking no mo' hands
everything i need come from those hands

tired & still grabbing grease, hum
while she makes her son royal onyx hands.

mama, how far am i
gone from home?

     //

do you know what it's like to live
on land who loves you back?

no need for geography
now, we safe everywhere.

point to whatever you please
& call it church, home, or sweet love.

paradise is a world where everything
is sanctuary & nothing is a gun.

here, if it grows it knows its place
in history. yesterday, a poplar

told me of old forest
heavy with fruits i'd call uncle

bursting red pulp & set afire
harvest of dark wind chimes.

after i fell from its limb
it bandaged me in sap.

     //

i loved a boy once & once he made me
a red dirge, skin casket, no burial.

left me to become a hum in a choir
of bug mouths. he was my pastor

in violet velvet, my night nurse
my tumor, my sick heart, my bad blood

all over his Tims. he needed me
so much he had to end me.

i was his fag sucked into ash
his lungs my final resting place.

my baby turned me to smoke
choked on my name 'til it was gone.

i was his secret until i wasn't
alive until not. outside our closet

i found a garden. he would love it
here. he could love me here.

//

dear brother from another
time, today some stars gave in

to the black around them
& i knew it was you.

my ace, my g, my fellow
kingdomless king

they've made you a boy
i don't know

replaced my friend
with a hashtag.

wish i could tell you
his hands are draped

from my neck, but his
shield is shaped like

a badge. i leave revenge
hopelessly to God.

//

last night's dream was a red June
filled with our mouths sticky

with sugar, we tiny teethed brown beasts
of corner stores, fingers always

dusted cheeto gold. do you remember
those yellow months? our calves burned

all day biking each other around on pegs
taking turns being steed & warrior

at the park we stormed like distant shores
our little ashy wars, shoes lit with blue sparks

those summers we chased anybody
who would say our names, jumped fences

just to prove we could jump, fingers stained
piff green with stank, riding around

barely old enough to ride around, dreaming
a world to conquer? i wish you ended me, Sweet Cain.

/ /

if we dream the old world
we wake up hands up.

sometimes we unfuneral a boy
who shot another boy to here

& who was once a reaper we make
a brother, a crush, a husband, a duet

of sweet remission. say the word
i can make any black boy a savior

make him a flock of ravens
his body burst into ebon seraphs.

this, our handcrafted religion.
we are small gods of redemption.

we dance until guilt turns to sweat.
we sweat until we flood & drown.

don't fret, we don't die. they can't kill
the boy on your shirt again.

//

the forest is a flock of boys
who never got to grow up

blooming into forever
afros like maple crowns

reaching sap-slow toward sky. watch
Forest run in the rain, branches

melting into paper-soft curls, duck
under the mountain for shelter. watch

the mountain reveal itself a boy.
watch Mountain & Forest playing

in the rain, watch the rain melt everything
into a boy with brown eyes & wet naps—

the lake turns into a boy in the rain
the swamp—a boy in the rain

the fields of lavender—brothers
dancing between the storm.

//

when i want to kiss you
i kiss the ground.

i shout down sirens.
they bring no safety.

my king turned my ache
my one turned into my nothing.

all last month was spent in bed
with your long gone name.

what good is a name
if no one answers back?

i know when the wind feels
as if it's made of hands

& i feel like i'm made of water
it's you trying to save me

from drowning in myself, but i can't
wed wind. i'm not water.

11

dear dear
my most distant love—

when i dream of you i wake
in a field so blue i drown.

if you were here, we could play
Eden all day, but fruit here

grows strange, i know before me
here lived something treacherous.

whose arms hold you now
after my paradise grew from chaos?

whose name do you make
thunder the room?

is he a good man?
does he know my face?

does he look like me?
do i keep him up at night?

/ /

how old am i? today, i'm today.
i'm as old as whatever light touches me.

some nights i'm new as the fire at my feet
some nights i'm a star, glamorous, ancient

& already extinguished. we citizens
of an unpopular heaven

& low-attended crucifixions. listen
i've accepted what i was given

be it my name or be it my ender's verdict.
when i was born, i was born a bull's-eye.

i spent my life arguing how i mattered
until it didn't matter.

who knew my haven
would be my coffin?

dead is the safest i've ever been.
i've never been so alive.

//

if you press your ear to the dirt
you can hear it hum, not like it's filled

with beetles & other low gods
but like a tongue rot with gospel

& other glories. listen to the dirt
crescendo a kid back.

come. celebrate. this
is everyday. everyday

holy. everyday high
holiday. everyday new

year. every year, days get longer.
time clogged with boys. the boys

O the boys. they still come
in droves. the old world

keeps choking them. our new one
can't stop spitting them out.

//

dear ghost i made

i was raised with a healthy fear of the dark.
i turned the light bright, but you just kept

being born, kept coming for me, kept being
so dark, i got sca . . . i was doing my job.

/ /

dear badge number

what did i do wrong?
be born? be black? meet you?

/ /

ask the mountainboy to put you on
his shoulders if you want to see

the old world, ask him for some lean
-in & you'll be home. step off him

& walk around your block.
grow wings & fly above your city.

all the guns fire toward heaven.
warning shots mince your feathers.

fall back to the metal-less side
of the mountainboy, cry if you need to.

that world of laws rendered us into dark
matter. we asked for nothing but our names

in a mouth we've known
for decades. some were blessed

to know the mouth.
our decades betrayed us.

            //

there, i drowned, back before, once.
there, i knew how to swim, but couldn't.

there, men stood by shore & watched me blue.
there, i was a dead fish, the river's prince.

there, i had a face & then didn't.
there, my mother cried over me, open casket

but i wasn't there. i was here, by my own
water, singing a song i learned somewhere

south of somewhere worse.
now, everywhere i am is

the center of everything. i must
be the lord of something.

what was i before? a boy? a son?
a warning? a myth? i whistled

now i'm the god of whistling.
i built my Olympia downstream.

     //

you are not welcome here. trust
the trip will kill you. go home.

we earned this paradise
by a death we didn't deserve.

i'm sure there are other heres.
a somewhere for every kind

of somebody, a heaven of brown
girls braiding on golden stoops

but here—
                how could i ever explain to you—

                someone prayed we'd rest in peace
                & here we are

                in peace   whole   all summer

dear white america

i've left Earth in search of darker planets, a solar system revolving too near a black hole. i've left in search of a new God. i do not trust the God you have given us. my grandmother's hallelujah is only outdone by the fear she nurses every time the blood-fat summer swallows another child who used to sing in the choir. take your God back. though his songs are beautiful, his miracles are inconsistent. i want the fate of Lazarus for Renisha, want Chucky, Bo, Meech, Trayvon, Sean & Jonylah risen three days after their entombing, their ghost re-gifted flesh & blood, their flesh & blood re-gifted their children. i've left Earth, i am equal parts sick of your *go back to Africa* & *i just don't see race*. neither did the poplar tree. we did not build your boats (though we did leave a trail of kin to guide us home). we did not build your prisons (though we did & we fill them too). we did not ask to be part of your America (though are we not America? her joints brittle & dragging a ripped gown through Oakland?). i can't stand your ground. i'm sick of calling your recklessness the law. each night, i count my brothers. & in the morning, when some do not survive to be counted, i count the holes they leave. i reach for black folks & touch only air. your master magic trick, America. now he's breathing, now he don't. abra-cadaver. white bread voodoo. sorcery you claim not to practice, hand my cousin a pistol to do your work. i tried, white people. i tried to love you, but you spent my brother's funeral making plans for brunch, talking too loud next to his bones. you took one look at the river, plump with the body of boy after girl after sweet boi & ask *why does it always have to be about race?* because you made it that way! because you put an asterisk on my sister's gorgeous face! call her pretty (for a black girl)! because black girls go missing without so much as a whisper of where?! because there are no amber alerts for amber-skinned girls! because Jordan boomed. because Emmett whistled. because Huey P. spoke. because Martin preached. because black boys can always be too loud to live. because it's taken my papa's & my grandma's time, my father's time, my mother's time, my aunt's time, my uncle's time, my brother's & my sister's time . . . how much time do you want for your progress? i've left Earth to find a place where my kin can be safe, where black people ain't but people the same color as the good, wet earth, until that means something, until then i bid you well, i bid you war, i bid you our lives to gamble with no more. i've left Earth & i am touching everything you beg your telescopes to show you. i'm giving the stars their right names. & this life, this new story & history you cannot steal or sell or cast overboard or hang or beat or drown or own or redline or shackle or silence or cheat or choke or cover up or jail or shoot or jail or shoot or jail or shoot or ruin

this, if only this one, is ours.

dinosaurs in the hood

let's make a movie called *Dinosaurs in the Hood*.
Jurassic Park meets *Friday* meets *The Pursuit of Happyness*.
there should be a scene where a little black boy is playing
with a toy dinosaur on the bus, then looks out the window
& sees the *T. rex*, because there has to be a *T. rex*.

don't let Tarantino direct this. in his version, the boy plays
with a gun, the metaphor: black boys toy with their own lives
the foreshadow to his end, the spitting image of his father.
nah, the kid has a plastic brontosaurus or triceratops
& this is his proof of magic or God or Santa. i want a scene

where a cop car gets pooped on by a pterodactyl, a scene
where the corner store turns into a battleground. don't let
the Wayans brothers in this movie. i don't want any racist shit
about Asian people or overused Latino stereotypes.
this movie is about a neighborhood of royal folks—

children of slaves & immigrants & addicts & exile—saving their town
from real ass dinosaurs. i don't want some cheesy, yet progressive
Hmong sexy hot dude hero with a funny, yet strong, commanding
Black girl buddy-cop film. this is not a vehicle for Will Smith
& Sofia Vergara. i want grandmas on the front porch taking out raptors

with guns they hid in walls & under mattresses. i want those little spitty
screamy dinosaurs. i want Cecily Tyson to make a speech, maybe two.
i want Viola Davis to save the city in the last scene with a black fist afro pick
through the last dinosaur's long, cold-blood neck. But this can't be
a black movie. this can't be a black movie. this movie can't be dismissed

because of its cast or its audience. this movie can't be metaphor
for black people & extinction. This movie can't be about race.
this movie can't be about black pain or cause black pain.
this movie can't be about a long history of having a long history with hurt.
this movie can't be about race. nobody can say nigga in this movie

who can't say it to my face in public. no chicken jokes in this movie.
no bullet holes in the heroes. & no one kills the black boy. & no one kills
the black boy. & no one kills the black boy. besides, the only reason
i want to make this is for the first scene anyway: little black boy
on the bus with his toy dinosaur, his eyes wide & endless

his dreams possible, pulsing, & right there.

it won't be a bullet

becoming a little moon—brightwarm in me one night.
thank god. i can go quietly. the doctor will explain death
& i'll go practice.

in the catalogue of ways to kill a black boy, find me
buried between the pages stuck together
with red stick. ironic, predictable. look at me.

i'm not the kind of black man who dies on the news.
i'm the kind who grows thinner & thinner & thinner
until light outweighs us, & we become it, family
gathered around my barely body telling me to go
toward myself.

last summer of innocence

there was Noella who knew i was sweet
but cared enough to bother with me

that summer when nobody died
except for boys from other schools

but not us, for which our mothers
lifted his holy name & even let us skip

some Sundays to go to the park
or be where we had no business being

talking to girls who had no interest
in us, who flocked to their new hips

dumb birds we were, nectar high
& singing all around them, preening

waves all day, white beater & our best
basketball shorts, the flyest shoes

our mamas could buy hot, line-up fresh
from someone's porch, someone's uncle

cutting heads round the corner cutting
eyes at the mothers of girls i pretended

to praise. i showed off for girls
but stared at my stupid, boney crew.

i knew the word for what i was
but couldn't think it. i played football

& believed its salvation, its antidote.
when Noella n 'nem didn't come out

& instead we turned our attention
to our wild legs, narrow arms & pig skin

i spent all day in my brothers' arms
& wanted that to be forever—

boy after boy after boy after boy
pulling me down into the dirt.

a note on Vaseline

praise the wet music of frantic palms
plastic toilet cushion & shiny fingers

your eyes shut, rebuilding how Sherrie bent
over in math or how Latrell walked around

after gym class, his underwear too small
& brand-new manhood undeniable. praise

the endless tub of grease. it's been the same
empty but not empty your whole life.

this very same Vaseline you're using to polish
your favorite body part was used by your mama

to slick her face when Ms. Lorelle from over
on Hague St. called her a frog-eyed bitch

back in '76, same grease your auntie used to make
a disco ball of her small, brown mouth when she

decided it was time to put it on Craig at the skating rink.
this same family-sized tub has been young

with all your elders, soothed Grandpa's gout
Grandma's fryer burns & Saturday morning bruises.

praise petroleum. how oily & blessed
the space between your fingers

supple blade between thumb & index
sends you to the guts of stars

remember this grip when men use the stuff
to prepare you for their want, when they leave you

throbbing, tender, & whistling from the wrong mouth
your bones replaced by yokes. you will never have enough

spit, & this is how men will want you always: slug slime
slick of a man, twitching tunnel of left hands.

a note on the phone app that tells me how far i am from other men's mouths

headless horsehung horsemen gallop to my gate
dressed in pictures stolen off Google

men of every tribe mark their doors in blood
No Fats, No Fems, No Blacks, Sorry, Just A Preference :)

i'm offered eight mouths, three asses, & four dicks before i'm given
a name, i offer my body to pictures with eyes

the three men who say they weigh more than 250 pounds
fill their profiles with pictures of landscapes, sunsets
write lovely sonnets about their lonely & good tongues

men with abs between their abs write *ask* or *probably not interested in you*

the boy down the street won't stop messaging me, i keep not responding
i thought about blocking him, but i don't want him to think i am dead

a man says *sup*, i say *chillin, you?* he says *word, so we fuckin or what?*
i never found out what *or what* was

ThEre Is ThIs OnE gUy WhO sPeLlS EvErYtHiNg LiKe ThIs

everyone on the app says they hate the app but no one stops

i sit on the train, eyeing men, begging myself
to talk to them

i sit on the face of a man i just met

he whispers his name into my lower mouth

i sing a song about being alone

& even the black guy's profile reads *sorry, no black guys*

imagine a tulip, upon seeing a garden full of tulips, sheds its petals in disgust, prays some bee will bring its pollen to a rose bush. imagine shadows longing for a room with light in every direction. you look in the mirror & see a man you refuse to love. small child sleeping near Clorox, dreaming of soap suds & milk, if no one has told you, you are beautiful & lovable & black & enough & so—you pretty you—am i.

O nigga O

the above is

a. the sound i made when he was most inside me
b. the word escaping his Georgia mouth to my yank ear
c. his face when he was most inside me
d. the original title of *Othello*

. . . nigga

somewhere a white boy is in his room, in the lunchroom, in the car, with his father, alone, in the dark, under his breath, as a battle cry, with the song, only with his white friends, in his lover's ear, when he's 8, when he's 40, as he comes, as tradition, as the punch line, just to try it nigga[1]

1. he means all of us

at the down-low house party

don't expect no nigga to dance.
we drink hen, hold the wall

graze an elbow & pray it last forever.
everybody wants to touch a nigga, but don't.

we say *wats gud* meaning *i could love you until my jaw*
is but memory, we say *yo* meaning *let my body*

be a falcon's talon & your body be the soft innards of goats
but we mostly say nothing, just sip

some good brown trying to get drunk
with permission. sometime between here

& being straight again, some sweet
boned, glittering boi shows up, starts voguing & shit

his sharp hips pierce our desire, make our mouths water
& water & we call him *faggot* meaning *bravery*

faggot meaning *often dream*
of you, flesh damp & confused for mine

faggot meaning *Hail the queen! Hail the queen!*
faggot meaning *i been waited ages to dance with you.*

bare

for you i'd send my body to battle
my body, let my blood sing of tearing

itself apart, hollow cords
of white knights' intravenous joist.

love, I want & barely know how
to do much else. don't speak to me

about raids you could loose on me
the clan of rebel cells who thirst

to watch their home burn. love
let me burn if it means you

& i have one night with no barrier
but skin. this isn't about danger

but about faith, about being wasted
on your name. if love is a room

of broken glass, leave me to dance
until my feet are memory.

if love is a hole wide enough
to be God's mouth, let me plunge

into that holy dark & forget
the color of light. love, stay

in me until our bodies forget
what divides us, until your hands

are my hands & your blood
is my blood & your name

is my name & his & his

seroconversion

i.

two boys are in bed on a Tuesday afternoon &
neither knows the other's name for they just met
this morning on their phones & were 1.2 miles
from each other & so now lay together & one
boy reaches his bare hand inside the other, pulls
out a parade of fantastic beasts: lions with house
fly wings, fish who thrive in boiling water, horses
who've learned to sleep while running. he pulls
out beasts, one by one, until all the magic is gone
& the gutted boy turns into a pig. pig boy & boy
spend a day with no language & the boy, hearing
no protest, splits the pig open & crawls right in,
& the pig, not one to protest, divides in half &
lets the boy think he split him. when they're
finished, they dress & part & never forget what
happened. how can they? the boy's still covered
in pig blood, the pig's still split.

ii.

the god of shovels visits the god of soil.
obvious things happen. in the hole made
out of the god of soil, the god of shovels
places a red flower given to him by the
god of shadows. it's not until the god of
shovels is leaving that the soil god notices
the shovel god's back covered in red,
honeyhot thorns, then looks at his thighs,
sees little ruby tongues sprouting.

iii.

there was a boy made of bad teeth & a boy made of
stale bread & together they were a hot mouth
making mush out of yeasty stones & in the end the
one made of bad teeth walked away broken jawed,
sick with hunger & the one made of stale bread
walked away half of himself, his softness proved a
lie & what remains left for unparticular birds.

iv.

on a quiet day, filled with not enough questions, a
prince demands the gates opened, for a fair
princess has come to see him. when the gates
come up, an endless flood of soldiers bum-rush
the town, turning everything to fire: the homes,
the husbands, the places where the people learned
to dance. the princess brings the prince before
her, he looks at her with eyes that ask *how could
you?* & she looks back with eyes that say *they said i
was a princess, that I'd come to see you, but you assumed
flowers when i prefer a bouquet of swords.*

v.

one day, the boy with a difficult name
laid with a boy who shall remain
nameless in the sun & they rolled around
waiting for something to burn. the next
day, the boy with the difficult name
woke up in a blue sweat, walked the rim
of the lake & though nothing burned,
something was growing from ashes, for
mosquitos flew away from his skin, ticks
latched onto his ankle & turned to
smoke, weeds & willows bowed green
spines to him & he swore he heard the
dirt singing his name

saying it right

fear of needles

instead of getting tested
you take a blade to your palm
hold your ear to the wound

recklessly

for Michael Johnson

the bloodprison leads to prison

    jail doubles as quarantine

chest to chest, men are silent

    you're under arrest, under a spell

are you on treatment? PrEP? (*wats dat?*)

    venom:sin:snake:cocksize

        i got the cellblock blues

    the diagnosis is judgment enough

you got the suga? the clap? the mumps?

    i say *mercy, danger* & white boys hear what they want

it was summer & everyone wanted to be in love

    i been drankin, I been drankin

i just wanna dance with somebody

    it could all be so simple

        but you don't know my name

    don't ask. don't tell

many stories about queerness are about shame

    . . . shall not lie (with mankind) . . .

    i got the cell count blues

inside a cell: a man/inside his cells: a man

    can you keep a secret?

a history of blood: from sacrament to sentence

    the red the white the blue of my veins

//

singing recklessly out of a boy's/throat, driving recklessly with boy/hands, lay my mouth on a man/as you lay a boy/into bed/ruin a boy like a boy/running recklessly/ in the rain in Easter white/as boys do/eating recklessly with a boy's/hunger, praising recklessly whatever was near/knelling/recklessly with a boy's knees/in front of convenient gods/when morning came & still i was/recklessly a boy's throat/ until he was done & everywhere on my body was a boy's throat/yes, i was his if only once/& i was his/as well & i was/everywhere, like a god/or a virus & i was everything/required of me & i was anything/but tame/& so, so long from then/ i stand in the deepest part of night/singing recklessly, calling/what must feast/ to feast.

//

- a love story -

he came/over

& then he left

but he stayed

/ /

as smoke from the lips
cycles into the nose

as the car filled with bass
niggas & smoke smokes your hair

as the car rolls into his garage
as you become a kind of garage

as the skin breaks as the skin do
as salt overwhelms

your simple palate as you sing
salt devotion as salt

gives way to salt as you are
a body boiled down to desire

as a noun, as to say *desire*
all over my face or say *desire*

coming down my leg
or *desire feels cold*

which lets you know
desire was warm recently

shot from inside a body
into a body, strange

little birth, happy death
ritual, sweet lord

i've seen thy wrath
& it taste like sugar

lay thy merciful hand
around my neck

//

```
it's not a death sentence anymore
it's not   death              anymore
it's                            more
it's     a       sentence
         a       sentence


        / /
```

i told him what
happened to my body

but all he could hear
was light falling
between my legs

next time a man comes
over, i'll cut the veins
out my arms, arrange them

like cooked linguine
on the kitchen table

in the shape of a boy's face
& say *here's what happened*

   //

in our blood

men hold each other

like they'll never let go

& then they let go

elegy with pixels & cum

for Javier "Kid Chocolate" Bravo

they won't let you stay dead, kid.

today's update: your dead flesh stitched digital, kid.

this gravestone: no lilies, a dick pic, no proof you were someone's, kid.

ghost plunge into a still alive boy, make him scream like a bleeding kid.

did they dress or undress you for burial, kid?

your mother watches you choke a man into pleasure, can't look away, just misses her kid.

men gather in front of screens to jerk & mourn, kid.

don't know your real name, kid.

you fuck like an animal, you die like an animal, kid.

i have the same red shadow running through my veins, kid.

in my blood, a little bit of your blood, almost siblings, some bad father's kids.

did you know how many ways you can relate to a ghost, kid?

someone misses your laugh, not just the way you filled asses & screens, kid.

i bet they had a pastor who didn't know you do your eulogy, kid.

they turn our funerals into lessons, kid.

they say blood & everyone flinches, kid.

they say blood & watch us turn to dust, kid.

they want us quiet, redeemed, or dead already, kid.

they want us hard, tunnel-eyed, & bucking, kid.

they want us to fuck more than they want us to exist, kid.

they want us to know god or be god, kid.

how close was death to orgasm, kid?

how did it feel to feel everything, then become a thing that can't feel, kid?

did a boy kiss what was left of you, kid?

did he flood the church with his mourning, kid?

was he the rain & you the ark, kid?

did he make a new sea to miss you, kid?

were you a fish swimming in his grief, kid? did you float?

litany with blood all over

i am telling you something   i got blood on the brain

              the prettiest fish are poisonous
              & same is true for men

test results say i talk too much

      test results say i ask none of the right questions

            test results have the blues

test results say i'm a myth
         proven true & by effect boring—Zeus proved just a boy
                                   playing with the lights

test results say my name
         is not my name & test results say my name
                      is banned from the radio

the test results say i am the father
      of my own end

          & i am
                  a deadbeat

i let the blood
raise my boy

i let the blood
bury him too

i let the blood do what i have always failed to do
& end the boy for good

blood & its endless screaming
or singing
or whatever people do when their village burns

again the blood & its clever songs

All
i
Desire
Surrenders

Have
i no
Venom?

again i have too many words for sadness

i touched the stove & the house burned down
i touched the boy & now i have his name

our bloodwedding—our bloodfuneral

i'm his new wife at dusk & by morning i'm his widow

he left me his blood
& though he is not dead
i miss my husband

i hate my husband
        he left me with child

                i cut his awful seed out of me
                    but it always grows back

    the child comes half-dead calls me mother then dies
           & joins his brothers

  my veins—rivers of my drowned children
  my blood thick with blue daughters

my blood

          my blood
his blood   my blood   his blood

             my blood

      his blood
    my blood
                 my blood
   his blood his blood
my blood my blood
          my blood my blood
his blood his blood my blood his blood
blood   my blood my blood
  my blood his blood
his blood his blood
  my blood my blood my blood
  his blood his blood
  my blood his blood his blood my blood his blood
my blood my blood his blood my blood my blood
his blood   my blood
blood my blood his blood my blood his blood my blood
  his blood my blood his blood his my blood
his blood my blood his blood my blood
blood blood his blood his blood his blood his blood
blood my blood my blood my blood his blood his blood my blood
my blood his blood his blood his blood his blood his blood
my blood   his blood my blood my blood his blood
his blood my blood his blood his blood
my blood his blood his my his blood blood
  my blood his his blood

his blood my blood his blood my blood his blood my blood his blood my blood his blood my blood

his blood my blood his blood his blood my blood his blood my blood his blood my blood my blood

his blood his blood my blood his blood his blood my blood his blood my blood his blood my blood

my blood his blood my blood his blood my blood my blood his blood my blood my blood his blood

his blood my blood his blood my blood his blood his blood my blood his blood my blood his blood

my blood his blood my blood his blood my blood his blood my blood his blood my blood his blood

it began right here

a humbling at my knees. i let him record me, wanted to
watch me be monster, didn't know he'd leave me

with vultures grazing my veins. me: dead lion who keeps
dying. him: flies who won't leave my blood alone. the devil

sleeps in my eyes, my tongue, my dick, my liver, my heart.
everywhere blood is he sleeps. & i knew before i knew

& can't tell you how. ghosts have always been real
& i apprentice them now. they say it's not a death sentence

like it used to be. but it's still life. i will die in this bloodcell.
i'm learning to become all the space i need. i laughed today.

for a second I was unhaunted. i was the sun, not light
from some dead star. i was before. i was negative. but i'm not.

i am a house swollen with the dead, but still a home.
the bed where it happened is where i sleep.

crown

i don't know how, but surely, & then again
the boy, who is not a boy, & i, who is barely
me by now, meld into a wicked, if not lovely
beast, black lacquered in black, darker
star, sky away from the sky, he begs, or
is it i beg him to beg, for me to open
which i do, which i didn't need to be asked
but the script matters, audition & rehearse
the body—a theatre on the edge of town
chitlin' circuit opera house, he runs a hand
praise the hand, over me, still red with hot
sauce, is that what it is? his hands, jeweled
in, what? what could it be? what did he pull
from me? a robin? a wagon? our red child?

//

pulled from me: a robin, a wagon, our red child
with dead red bird in his hands, dead child
in red coffin on wheels, parade out of me
second line up the needle & into the vial
all the children i'll never have, dead in me
widow father, sac fat with mourning, dusk
is the color of my blood, blood & milk
colored, chalk virus, the boy writes on me
& erases, the boy claps me between
his hands & i break apart like glitter
like coke, was there coke that night?
my nose went white then red all over
thin red river flowing down my face
my blood jumped to ask him to wade.

//

my blood got jumped, ask him to wait
before he gives me the test results, give
me a moment of not knowing, sweet
piece of ignorance, i want to go back
to the question, sweet if of yesterday
bridge back to maybe, lord bring me
my old blood's name, take away
the crown of red fruit sprouting
& rotting & sprouting & rotting.
in me: a garden of his brown mouth
his clean teeth, his clean answer
phantom hiding behind a red curtain
& i would sing if not for blood in my throat
if my blood was not a moat.

//

if my blood was not a moat, i'd have a son
but i kingdom myself, watch the castle turn
to exquisite mush. look at how easy bones
turn to grits how the body becomes effigy.
would have a daughter but i am only
the mother of my leaving. i sit on jungle gym
crying over other people's children, black
flowers blooming where my tears fall.
bees commune at their lips, then
turn them to stone. as expected.
my blood a river named medusa. every man
i touch turns into a monument. i put
flowers at their feet, their terrible stone feet.
they grow wings, stone wings, & crumble.

//

they grow wings, stoned wings, crumble
& fall right out my body, my little darlings.
i walk & leave a trail of my little never-
no-mores. my little angels, their little feathers
clogging the drain, little cherubs drowning
right in my body, little prayers bubbling
at the mouth, little blue-skinned joys
little dead jokes, little brown-eyed can'ts
my nursery of nunca, family portrait
full of grinning ghosts, they look just like me
proud papa of pity, forever uncle, father
figure figured out of legacy, doomed daddy.
look at my children, skipping toward the hill
& over the hill: a cliff, a fire, an awful mouth.

//

& over the hill: a cliff, a fire, the awful mouth
of an awful river, a junkyard, a church made
from burnt churches—place for prayer
for those who have forgotten how to pray.
i stand by the river, the awful one, dunk
my head in the water & scream
for my river-bottom heirs—this is prayer
right? i fall & i drown & i trash & i burn
& i dunk my head in the water & i
call the children drowned in my blood
to come home—this is the right prayer?
lord, give me a sign, red & octagonal.
god bless the child that's got his own.
god bless the father who will have none.

//

god bless the father who will have none
to call him father, god bless the lonely
god who will create nothing. but there's
pills for that. but the pills cost too much.
& the womb cost money to rent.
but who will let you fill them with seed
from a tree of black snakes? but i didn't know
what he was bringing to me. but he
told me he was negative. but he wasn't
aware of the red witch spinning
in his blood. but he tasted so sweet.
sweet as a child's smile. sweet as a dream
filled with children who look just like you
you know: black, chubby, beaming, dying.

       //

you know: black, chubby, beaming, dying
of hunger, dying on the news, dying to forget
the news, he came to me like that. we were
almost brothers, almost blood, then we were.
good god, we made a kind of family—in my veins
my sons-brothers sleep, sisters-daughters
name each cell royal, home, untouchable.
in every dream, i un- my children:
untuck them into bed, unkiss their lil wounds
unteach them how to pray, unwake in the night
to watch their little chests rise & fall, unname
them, tuck them back into their mothers
& i wake up in bed with him—his red, dead, gift
i don't know how, but surely, & then again.

blood hangover

if there's a cure for this

                                          i want it

                  if there's a remedy
i'll run
        all the time
                         let it out

'cause

i've got the sweetest hangover
        i don't want

yeah i want to get

                      over

              ooh no cure
              i need cure
        i need cure
i don't need
        sweet lovin'

call the doctor
              momma
        don't call preacher

                  no i need it
            i don't want it
            i love need

love
a cure for this

        i don't want it
i want it

            if there's a cure for this

      sweet sweet sweet sweet
      sweet sweet sweet sweet
      sweet sweet sweet sweet

1 in 2

On February 23rd, 2016, the CDC released a study estimating 1 in 2 black men who have sex with men will be diagnosed with HIV in their lifetime.

the cells of you heard a tune you could not hear. you memorized & masqueraded, karaoked without knowing. you went in for a routine test & they told you what you were made of:

-honey spoiled into mead
-lemon mold
-broken proofs
-traffic tickets
-unidentified shard
-a shy, red moon
-a book of antonyms
-the book of job
-a lost child unaware of its name

you knew it would come to this, but then it actually came.

//

away to the red lake
to dance in the red waves

oh sugar boys, my
choir candy, wade slow

& forever, dip a toe
& red water will crawl

toward your neck
come on, dive in

or be swallowed
the water wants

to meet you, why
not on such a pretty

night, with the shore's
burgundy foam

teething toward your feet
like wine out for blood

& the sky above
dark as a nigga

who once told you
you cute & don't worry

  //

he, who smelled coffee sweet & cigarillo blue
entered me, who knew better but _____.
he, who in his wake left shredded tarot,
threw back his head & spewed light from every opening
& in me, light fell on a door, & in the door
a me i didn't know & knew, the now me
whose blood blacks & curls back like paper
near an open flame. i walked toward the door
as i walked away from the door. when i met me
in the middle, nothing grand happened.
a rumor made its way around my body.

  //

if you trace the word *diagnosis* back enough
you'll find *destiny*

   trace it forward, find *diaspora*

is there a word for the feeling prey
feel when the teeth finally sink
after years of waiting?

plague & *genocide* meet on a line in my body

i cut open my leg & it screamed

every day is a funeral & a miracle

on the bad nights, i wake to my mother
shoveling dirt down my throat
i scream mom! i'm alive! i'm alive!
but it just sounds like dirt

if i try to get up, she brings the shovel down
saying i miss you so much, my sweetest boy

    / /

my grandma doesn't know
        so don't tell her
if you see her with this poem

      burn it, burn her
burn whatever you must
        how do you tell a woman

who pretends you are just
        having trouble finding a wife
that once, twice, daily, a man

      enters you, how your blood
smells like a hospital, graveyard
        or a morgue left in the sun

    / /

hallelujah! today i rode
past five police cars
& i can tell you about it

now, what
to do with my internal
inverse, just how
will i survive the little
cops running inside
my veins, hunting
white blood cells &
bang bang
i'm dead

//

today, Tamir Rice
tomorrow, my liver
today, Rekia Boyd
tomorrow, the kidneys
today, John Crawford
tomorrow, my lungs

some of us are killed
in pieces, some of us all at once

//

do i think someone created AIDS?
maybe. i don't doubt that
anything is possible in a place
where you can burn a body
with less outrage than a flag

//

~~hallelujah! today~~
~~i did not think~~
~~about my blood~~

//

what is the shape of my people's salvation?

name a thing that can't be made a weapon?

can you point in the direction of the doctor?

witch or medical, no matter.

i got this problem: i was born

black & faggoty

      they sent a boy
      when the bullet missed.

      //

look, i'm not going to manufacture
any more sadness. it happened.
it's happening.

America might kill me before i get the chance.
my blood is in cahoots with the law.
but today i'm alive, which is to say

i survived yesterday, spent it
ducking bullets, some
flying toward me & some
trying to rip their way out.

not an elegy

how long

    does it take

a story

    to become

a legend?

how long before

    a legend

becomes

    a god or

forgotten?

ask the rain

    what it was

like to be the river

then ask the river

    who it drowned.

    //

i am sick of writing this poem
but bring the boy. his new name

his same old body. ordinary, black
dead thing. bring him & we will mourn
until we forget what we are mourning.

is that what being black is about?
not the joy of it, but the feeling

you get when you are looking
at your child, turn your head
then, poof, no more child.

that feeling. that's black.

     //

think: once, a white girl
was kidnapped & that's the Trojan War.

later, up the block, Troy got shot
& that was Tuesday. are we not worthy

of a city of ash? of 1,000 ships
launched because we are missed?

i demand a war to bring the dead child back.

i at least demand a song.   a head.

     //

if i must call this their fate
i know the color of God's face.

     //

do you expect
me to dance

when every day someone
who looks like everyone

i love is in a gun fight
armed with skin?

look closely
& you'll find a funeral

frothing in the corners
of my mouth, my mouth

hungry for prayer
to make it all a lie.

reader, what does it
feel like to be safe? white?

how does it feel
to dance when you're not

dancing away the ghost?
how does joy taste

when it's not followed
by *will come in the morning?*

reader, it's morning again
& somewhere, a mother

is pulling her hands
across her seed's cold shoulders

kissing what's left
of his face. where

is her joy? what's she
to do with a child

who'll spoil soon?
& what of the child?

what was their last dream?
who sang to them

while the world closed
into dust?

what cure marker did we just kill?
what legend did we deny

their legend? i have no more
room for grief.

it's everywhere now.
listen to my laugh

& if you pay attention
you'll hear a wake.

> //

prediction: the cop will walk free
prediction: the boy will still be dead

> //

to begin again i'd give my tongue
a cop's tongue too.

> //

a boy i was a boy with took his own life.
i forgot black boys leave that way too.

have i spent too much time worrying
about boys killing each other & being killed

that i forgot the ones who do it
with their own hands? is that not black

on black violence? a mother tucks her son
into earth, is it not the same plot?

i have no words to bring him back, i am
not magic enough. people at the funeral

wondered what made him do it. people said
he saw something. i think that's it. he saw something

what? the world? a road?

trees? a pair of ivory hands?

    his reflection?

his son's?

    a river saying his name?

a note on the body

your body still your body
your arms still wing
your mouth still a gun

      you tragic, misfiring bird

you have all you need to be a hero
don't save the world, save yourself

you worship too much & you worship too much

when prayer doesn't work: dance, fly, fire

this is your hardest scene
when you think the whole sad thing might end

but you live   oh, you live

everyday you wake you raise the dead

      everything you do is a miracle

you're dead, america

i fed your body to the fish
traded it at lunch for milk

i know where they buried you
'cause it's my mouth

they tell me *bootstraps*
& i spit up a little leather

they tell me *Christ*
but you don't have black friends

during the anthem
i hum "Niggas in Paris"

i cha cha slide over the flag
c-walk on occasion

i put a spell on you
it called for 3/5s of my blood

apple pie, red
bones & a full moon

but instead i did it
in the daylight, wanting you

to see me ending you
stupid stupid me

i know better than to fuck
with a recipe

i don't make chicken
when i don't have eggs

look at what i did: on the tv
the man from tv

is gonna be president
he has no words

& hair beyond simile
you're dead, america

& where you died
grew something worse—

crop white as the smile
of a man with his country on his side

a gun on his other

        //

tomorrow, i'll have hope

tomorrow, i can shift the wreckage

& find a seed

i don't know what will grow

i've lost my faith in this garden

the bees are dying

the water poisons whole cities

but my honeyed kin

those brown folks who make

up the nation of my heart

only allegiance i stand for

realer than any god

for them i bury whatever

this country thought it was

strange dowry

bloodwife they whisper when i raise my hand for another rum coke
      the ill savior of my veins proceeds me, my digital honesty about what
queer bacteria dotted my blood with snake mist & shatter potions
      they stare at my body, off the app, unpixelated & poison pretty flesh
men leave me be, i dance with the ghost i came here with
      a boy with three piercings & muddy eyes smiles & disappears into the strobes
the light spits him out near my ear, against my slow & practiced grind
      he could be my honey knight, the hand to break me apart like dry bread
there is a dream where we are horses that neither one of us has
      for five songs my body years of dust fields, his body rain
in my ear he offers me his bed promise live stock meat salt lust brief marriage
      i tell him the thing i must tell him, of the boy & the blood & the magic trick
me too   his strange dowry   vein brother-wife   partner in death juke
      what a strange gift to need, the good news that the boy you like is dying too
we let the night blur into cum wonder & blood hallelujah
      in the morning, seven emails: meeting, junk, rejection, junk, blood work results
i put on a pot of coffee, the boy stirs from whatever he dreams
      & it's like that for a while, me & that boy lived a good little life for a bit
in the mornings, we'd both take a pill, then thrash

tonight, in Oakland

i did not come here to sing you blues.
lately, i open my mouth

& out comes marigolds, yellow plums.
i came to make the sky a garden.

give me rain or give me honey, dear lord.
the sky has given us no water this year.

i ride my bike to a boy, when i get there
what we make will not be beautiful

or love at all, but it will be deserved.
i've started seeking men to wet the harvest.

come, tonight i declare we must move
instead of pray. tonight, east of here

two men, one dressed in what could be blood
& one dressed in what could be blood

before the wound, meet & mean mug
& God, tonight, let them dance! tonight

guns don't exist. tonight, the police
have turned to their God for forgiveness.

tonight, we bury nothing, we serve a God
with no need for shovels, God with a bad hip

& a brother in jail. tonight, prisons turn to tulips
& prisoner means *one who dances in a yellow field.*

tonight, let everyone be their own lord.
let wherever two people stand be a reunion

of ancient lights. let's waste the moon's marble glow
shouting our names to the stars until we are

the stars. O, precious God! O, sweet black town!
i am drunk & i thirst. when i get to the boy

who lets me practice hunger with him
i won't give him the name of your newest ghost

i will give him my body & what he does with it
is none of my business, but i will say *look*

i made it a whole day, still, no rain
still, i am without exit wound

& he will say *tonight, i want to take you*
how the police do, unarmed & sudden.

little prayer

let ruin end here

let him find honey
where there was once a slaughter

let him enter the lion's cage
& find a field of lilacs

let this be the healing
& if not   let it be

dream where every black person is standing by the ocean

& we say to her
> *what have you done with our kin you swallowed?*

& she says
> *that was ages ago, you've drunk them by now*

& we don't understand

& then one woman, skin dark as all of us
> walks to the water's lip, shouts *Emmett*, spits

&, surely, a boy begins
> crawling his way to shore

Notes

"summer, somewhere" borrows language from Erykah Badu's "Jump Up in the Air (Stay There)," Lucille Clifton's "won't you celebrate with me" & Ocean Vuong's "Homewrecker."

"recklessly" is for Michael Johnson, who is imprisoned for allegedly not disclosing his HIV status to sexual partners. It uses lines from Beyoncé, Alicia Keys, Lauryn Hill, Whitney Houston & Jodeci. The section that begins "in our blood" draws inspiration & language from Jericho Brown.

"litany with blood all over" is after Richard Siken's "Litany in Which Certain Things Are Crossed Out."

"it began right here" borrows its title & opening line from the play *Mirrors in Every Corner* by Chinaka Hodge.

"blood hangover" is an erasure of Diana Ross's "Love Hangover."

Acknowledgments

Many thanks to the editors & staff of the following publications in which early versions of these poems have appeared:

Alice Blue Review, Ampersand Review, At Length, Blue Shift, BuzzFeed Reader, Granta, Gulf Coast, HEArt Journal, HocTok, IDK Magazine, Linebreak, Lit Hub, Narrative, The Paris-American, PEN America, Poetry, Prairie Schooner, Quarterly West, The Rumpus, Split This Rock's Poem of the Week, Vinyl Poetry.

"dear white america" & "dinosaurs in the hood" appear in *The BreakBeat Poets: New American Poetry in the Age of Hip-Hop* (Haymarket Books, 2015).

"last summer of innocence" was selected by Natasha Trethewey for *The Best American Poetry 2017* (Scribner, 2017).

"tonight, in Oakland" was featured on the Poetry Foundation's broadcast *Poetry Now* & was published on the Poetry Foundation's website.

Poems from this manuscript were granted a prize in the Avery Hopwood & Julie Hopwood Contest for 2016 at the University of Michigan.

Some of these poems were included in the chapbook *black movie* (Button Poetry, 2015).

//

Thank you, God.

Thank you Chris Abani for giving this book its first blessing. And thank you to D. A. Powell & Tracy K. Smith for blessing it along the way.

Thank you Jeff Shotts & the entire staff at Graywolf for your vision, support & brilliant work.

Thank you Parisa Ebrahimi & the staff at Chatto & Windus for your support & vision for the UK edition.

Thank you to Don Share & the Poetry Foundation, the McKnight Foundation, Bao Phi & the Loft Literary Center, the Millay Colony for the Arts, Cave Canem & VONA for the overwhelming support, love, encouragement & belief in the necessity of poetry.

Thank you to the faculty & writers at the University of Michigan MFA Program.

Thank you Fatimah Asghar, Hieu Minh Nguyen, Cam Awkward Rich & sam sax for reading these poems in their most infantile & vulnerable states: you are the authors of them as well. I love you immensely.

Thank you to the poets & otherworldly kin that keep me afloat & alive: Tish Jones, Nate Marshall, Jamila Woods, Franny Choi, Aaron Samuels, Angel Nafis, Morgan Parker, Derrick Austin, Airea D. Matthews, Phillip B. Williams, L. Lamar Wilson, Britteney Black Rose Kapri, Charif Shanahan & Saeed Jones.

Thank you to my great friends Thiahera Nurse, D'Allen White, Krysta Rayford, Kamia Watson, Cydney Edwards, Sofia Snow, Karl Iglesias, Dominique Chestand & Kelsey Van Ert.

Thank you Chris Walker, Amaud Johnson, Jan Mandell & Patricia Smith, my eternal teachers. Every poem I write is coded with your lessons.

Thank you Blaire White, my best friend & ace. Thank you for loving me even though you hate poetry.

Thank you to my amazing family, the Smiths, Henrys & Pattersons. Thank you mom, you are my number one hero & my proof of good. Thank you dad for passing down poetry through your blood. I am thankful you both turned an accident into a lifetime of love & support.

Thank you, reader. This is yours now.

DANEZ SMITH was born in Saint Paul, Minnesota, and is the author of *[insert] boy*, winner of the Kate Tufts Discovery Award and the Lambda Literary Award. Smith is the recipient of fellowships from Cave Canem, the McKnight Foundation, the National Endowment for the Arts, and VONA, and was awarded a Ruth Lilly and Dorothy Sargent Rosenberg Poetry Fellowship from the Poetry Foundation. A founding member of the Dark Noise Collective, and twice a finalist for the Individual World Poetry Slam, Smith lives in Minneapolis.

www.danezsmithpoet.com

The text of *Don't Call Us Dead* is set in Adobe Garamond Pro. Book design by Rachel Holscher. Composition by Bookmobile Design & Digital Publisher Services, Minneapolis, Minnesota. Manufactured by Versa Press on acid-free, 30 percent postconsumer wastepaper.